Vasavadatta.

KING PRADYOTA OF UJJAINI WAS A VAIN MONARCH.

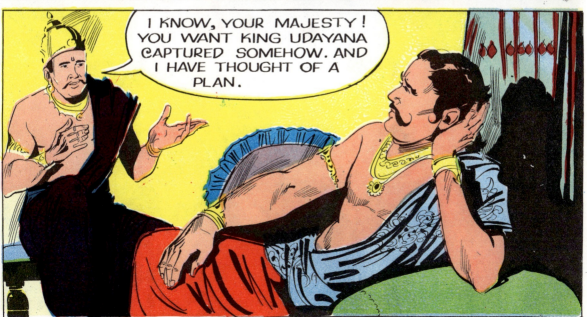

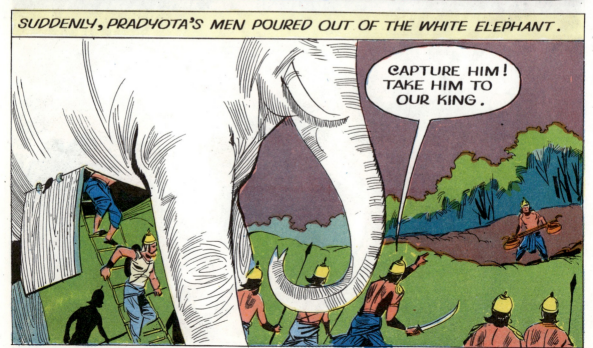

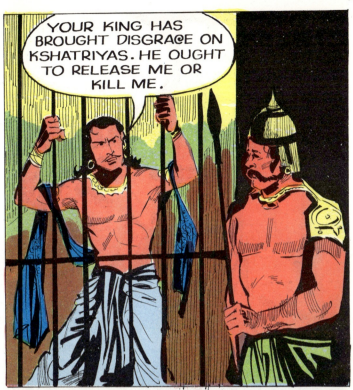

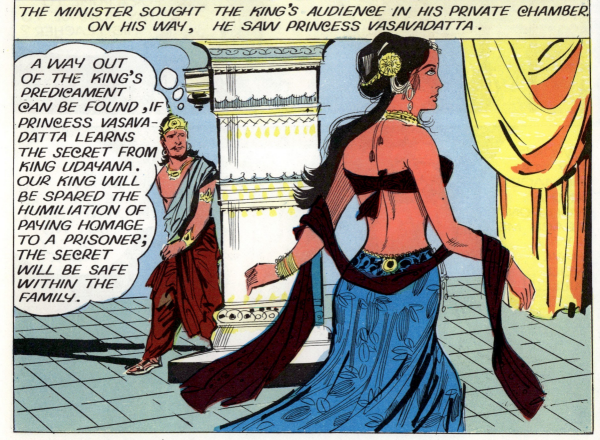

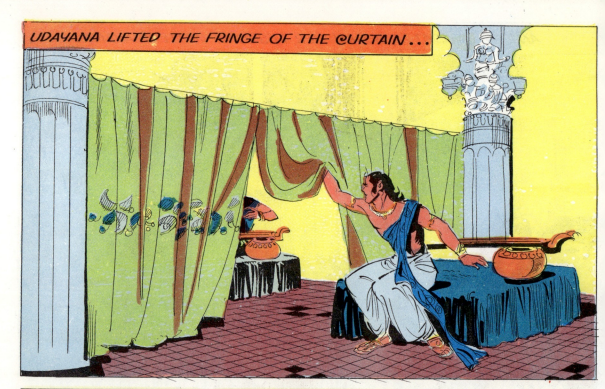

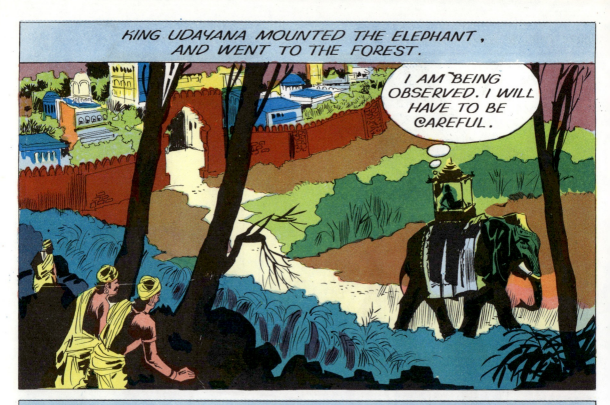

ON THE FOURTH NIGHT, KING PRADYOTA WAS AMUSING HIMSELF IN THE PALACE GARDEN.

UDAYANA WAS QUICK TO SEIZE HIS OPPORTUNITY.

PRINCESS! NOW IS THE TIME TO FLEE. BE QUICK.

VASAVADATTA ALSO MOUNTED THE ELEPHANT.

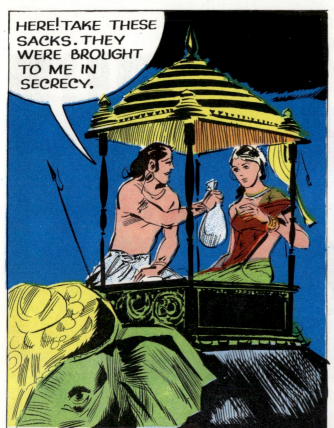